THE BOY WHO DARED TO BELIEVE

BY DAVID GILNA

ILLUSTRATIONS BY LAUREN TARPEY

Copyright © David Gilna, 2025

978-1-915502-97-1

All rights reserved. No part of this publication may be reproduced, distributed, or transmitted in any form or by any means, including photocopying, recording, or other electronic or mechanical methods, without the prior written permission of the author. Published in Ireland by Orla Kelly Publishing.

In a quiet suburban street lived a boy who loved to create.
He would paint, write, and perform every chance he got.

Learning lines from his favourite cartoons and shows, he would stand on a wooden memory box and perform for his teddy bears and toys.

Creating made him happy, as he dreamed of performing one day to a packed audience on the biggest stage.

But on one damp and windy Wednesday morning at school, his grumpy teacher, Mr. Snot, yelled at him from his desk,

"**Boy!**, what profession do you want to pursue when you grow up?"

The boy, quiet by nature, took a moment and smiled.

"I want to perform on the biggest stage the world has ever seen, entertain millions of people, and make them all laugh and forget about their worries," he said.

Mr. Snot stood up, his long and gangly arms pointing at the boy.

"**YOU** want to make people laugh for a living? My boy, don't make *me* laugh."

"Isn't your mother an accountant, a wizard at maths?" Mr. Snot snarled.

"Yes, she's the best at maths— better than you, I believe," the boy shot back. The classroom erupted in laughter and cheers.

"What did you say?" roared Mr. Snot.

"Sorry, Mr. Snot, I'm just telling the truth."

"My name is pronounced **Mr. Sot**, the 'n' is silent. I see you struggle with your English as well as your foolish dreams.

Step outside the classroom until you give me a real profession," he quipped.

The boy walked through the classroom with his head hanging low and opened the door, feeling defeated.

In the school corridors hung a giant tapestry of the great Irish Celtic legend, **Cú Chulainn**. The boy loved the stories his father used to tell him about the Irish gods and mythical creatures.

On days when he felt sad and alone, he would open his memory box with his mother and recall all the good times he had shared with his father when he was still alive.

"I miss you, Daddy," the boy cried.

Suddenly, the corridor lights began to flicker, and the tapestry burst into flames as a warrior stepped out of a time-traveling portal.

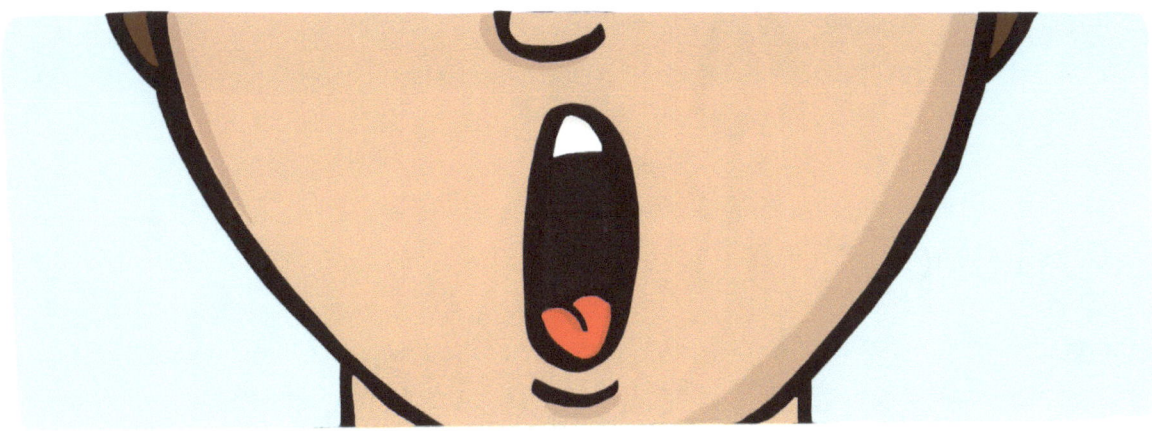

"I don't believe it," he whispered, trembling.

"Believe, my boy, for I am **Cú Chulainn**. We have a long journey ahead of us, and we must leave **now**," he bellowed.

"I'm frightened," said the boy.

Cú Chulainn bent down on one knee and whispered in his ear, "We all get frightened in life, my boy. But this is your **DESTINY**, and only you can decide your fate."

Cú Chulainn stood up, lifted the boy onto his shoulders, and, with his giant hounds, they bolted into the Celtic vortex,

waving goodbye to Jimmy the Caretaker as they t i m e - t r a v e l l e d through centuries.

The boy could hear the sound of the sea, and when he opened his eyes, he saw an island full of *colour* in the distance.

Cú Chulainn just smiled. "That is the land of the living souls, where spirits go when they leave us. It's a magical place filled with warmth and memories."

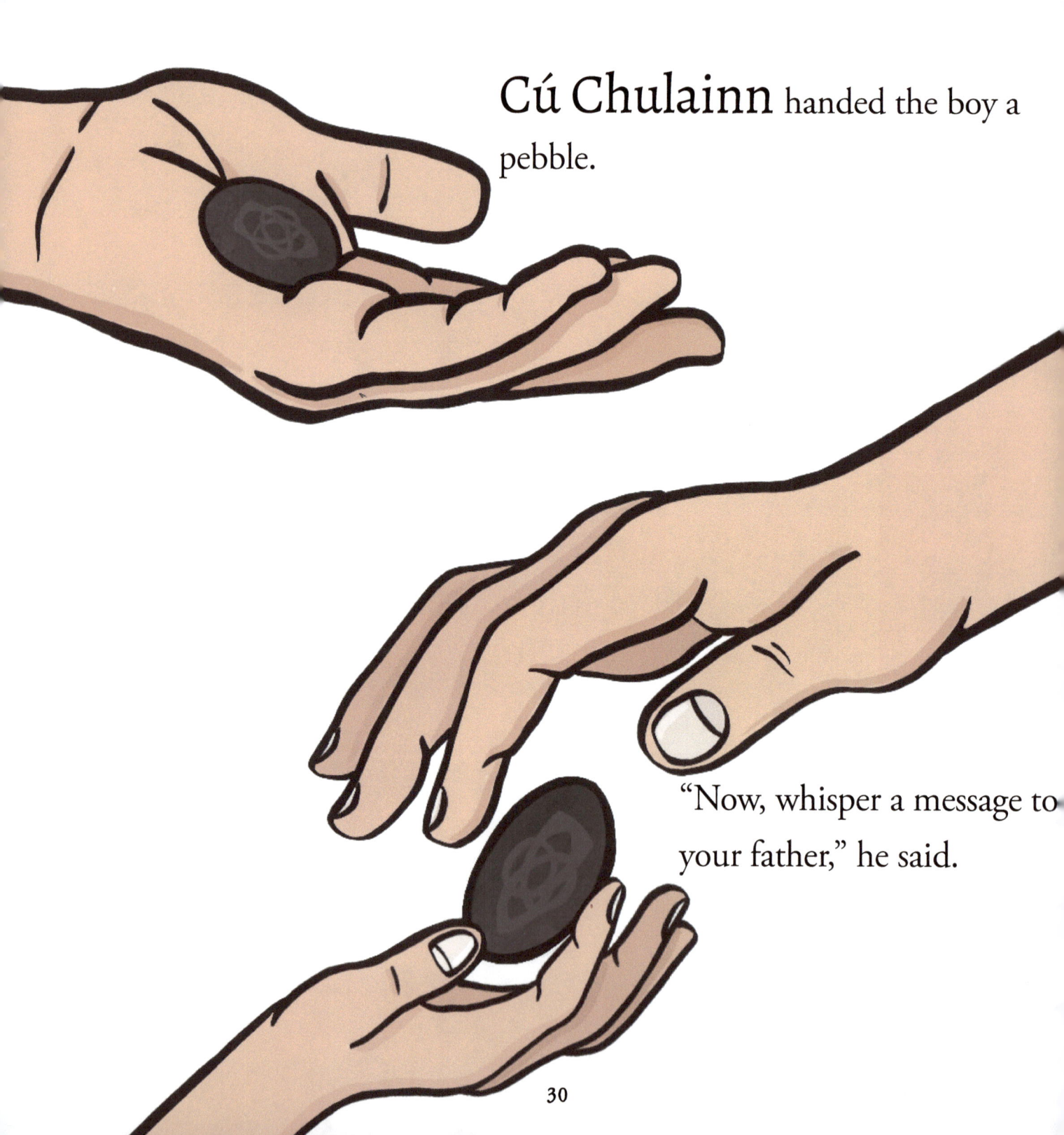

The boy closed his eyes and whispered to the pebble. When he opened them again, to his amazement, the pebble had turned to gold.

"Your message is now locked **FOREVER.**

With all your might and strength, throw it to the land of the living souls," roared **Cú Chulainn**.

The boy took a few steps back and, with a run and a jump, skimmed the pebble across the entire sea.

When it reached the land of the living souls, it erupted into fireworks. The boy smiled in wonder as the sky lit up. **Cú Chulainn** picked up a handful of sand and threw it into the air, the wind scattering it across the beach. "Just because we can't see the wind doesn't mean it's not there; we can feel it.

The spirits of our loved ones are always watching over us, willing us on through all of life's adversities."

The boy looked up at **Cú Chulainn** and smiled. "Thank you." Cú Chulainn gazed at him with pride.

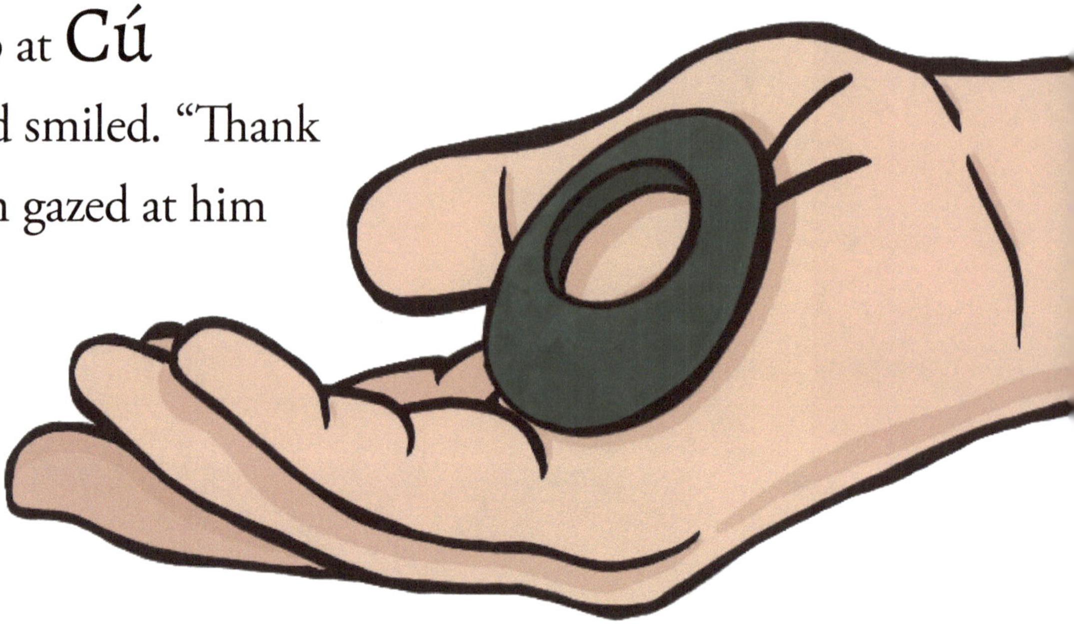

"There is a **warrior** inside of you," he said, handing him the future stone. "What is this?" asked the boy.

"A glimpse into your future path if you work hard and always fight for what you believe in," **Cú Chulainn** replied.

The boy cautiously examined the stone and suddenly found himself performing at The Olympia Theatre.

In the next moment, he was back in the school corridor, staring at the painting on the wall, but Cú Chulainn was nowhere to be seen. "Where is he?" he wondered.

Then, a hand popped out from the classroom door, beckoning him.

"Well boy, have you finally seen some sense?" snarled Mr. Snot.

"What profession do you wish to be when you grow up?"

The boy took a deep breath, closed his eyes, and, with power and projection, yelled, "I will be the best performer the world has ever seen!"

Mr. Snot's eyes went bloodshot with rage as the classroom cheered.

The boy quivered in fear,

and then, all of a sudden, the shadow of **Cú Chulainn** appeared.

A **roar** bellowed from his hounds.

Mr. Snot threw his papers into the air in panic and sprinted out the classroom door. The classroom erupted in cheers and delight.

That night, back at home, the boy performed a magical and wonderful one-man show for his mother in their living room, filled with love and imagination.